THOS EPISK OLS

?.6²

By
Dennis R. Maynard

www.Episkopols.com ☒
Dionysus Publications
Rancho Mirage, California

Dionysus Publications
49 Via Del Rossi
Rancho Mirage, California 92270

E-mail Orders & Comments:
Episkopols@aol.com
Telephone: 760-324-8589
www.Episkopols.com

Maynard, Dennis R. 1945
Those Episkopols

Library of Congress Catalog Card Number:
94-92277 ISBN 1-885985-02-9

Suggested Dewey Classification: 293.Ma

Suggested LC Classification: BX 5930.2.T56 1994
  Subjects:
    1. Episcopal Church – Doctrines
    2. Episcopal Church - Customs & Practices
    3. Christian Life

Cover Art by Diane Taylor

Twenty-fifth Printing 2010
100,000 Copies in Print

DEDICATION

To my wife Nancy Anne and our children

Jeannine Marie,
      Dennis Michael,
            Andrew Lockey,
                  And Kristen Anne

Some of the best Episkopols I know

OTHER BOOKS BY
DENNIS R. MAYNARD

FORGIVE AND GET YOUR LIFE BACK

This book teaches the forgiveness process to the reader. It's a popular resource for clergy and counselors to use to do forgiveness training. In this book, a clear distinction is made between forgiving, reconciling, and restoring the penitent person to their former position in our lives.

WHEN SHEEP ATTACK

Your rector is bullied, emotionally abused and then his ministry is ended. Your parish is left divided. Formerly faithful members no longer attend. This book is based on the case studies of twenty-five clergy who had just such an experience. What could have been done? What can you do to keep it from happening to you and your parish? Discussion questions are included that make it suitable for study groups.

THE MAGNOLIA SERIES

This series of fictional novels is based on the life of The Reverend Steele Austin. Father Austin receives an unlikely call to be rector of one of the most prestigious congregations in the state of Georgia. The people at historic old First Church have persevered to maintain a certain way of life. They have been just as diligent about seeing that their secrets of sex, power and money are kept well hidden.

You will fall in love with the young priest and his family as they seek to open the congregation and the community to people that do not meet the preconceived membership standards. You will also recognize several people in your own life. Take the first visit to Falls City, Georgia and you will come back again and again.

BEHIND THE MAGNOLIA TREE – BOOK ONE

Father Austin receives a cool welcome to historic First Church, but soon one of the leading members reveals a dark secret. Steele's life is threatened by the Klu Klux Klan. His own members plot to have him removed.

WHEN THE MAGNOLIA BLOOMS – BOOK TWO

One of Father Austin's close priest friends violates his marriage and ordination vows when he falls in love with another woman. The priest is then accused of murdering his own wife. Steele Austin is the only one that believes he is truly innocent. This page turner ends with an unexpected surprise.

PRUNING THE MAGNOLIA – BOOK THREE

The rector suspects that his administrator is embezzling funds from the parish. Before he can complete his investigation he finds himself under attack. Leading members in his congregation come to the defense of the administrator and convince the bishop that Father Austin is the thief.

THE PINK MAGNOLIA – BOOK FOUR

Steele opens a homeless shelter for teenagers that have been rejected by their own families because of their sexuality. Members of the Christian right immediately attack him. This book ends with one of the most suspense filled cliffhangers yet.

THE SWEET MAGNOLIA – BOOK FIVE

The young rector is anonymously presented with pictures that suggest that his own wife is an adulteress. His enemies threaten to make the pictures public if he doesn't resign.

THE MAGNOLIA AT SUNRISE – BOOK SIX
TO BE RELEASED DECEMBER, 2010

Father Austin takes his sabbatical time to examine his life's purpose. Still stinging from recent attacks, he is now uncertain if he wants to remain in the priesthood.

For discounted copies order on http://www.Episkopols.com.
All Doctor Maynard's books are also available through
Amazon.com or through your local bookstore.

FOREWORD

This book is written out of a profound love for The Episcopal Church. Writing it reaffirmed in me the very things that attracted me to this church five decades ago. The inspiring words and phrases in The Book of Common Prayer; our beautiful uplifting liturgies; our commitment to music that speaks both to the mind and the heart; and our respect for Holy Scripture that demands that it be treated with the scholarship that it deserves.

This is a church that does not seek its unity in like-mindedness, which can lead to small-mindedness. Our unity continues to be found in our common love for Jesus Christ and love and respect for our neighbor.

The Episcopal Church has been and continues to be the spiritual home of Presidents, Congressmen, Supreme Court Judges, College Presidents, and Corporate C.E.O.s. However, the vastness of our membership is found in the men and women who will not be mentioned in the history books, but are the very heart and soul of America.

The profound witness of the people of this church to the resurrection of Jesus Christ can be seen in the schools, colleges, hospitals, medical clinics, soup kitchens, and shelters for the homeless that reach to those in need not only in this land, but in distant places around the world.

This church for the most part has resisted the temptation for glossy advertisements and methods designed to pressure prospects into membership. She has chosen to be an invitational church with arms wide open to those who seek to follow Christ. From our great cathedrals in Washington, D.C., New York City and San Francisco, to the quaint churches in most every town and city of America, there is a congregation ready to welcome you.

Some have told me over the past decade that this book is timeless. There is a sense in which this might be true. As long as this book helps those seeking a church home fall in love with the things that make us uniquely Episcopalians, then it is without an expiration date. And if it can reignite love of this church in those who with the passing of the years have taken her for granted, then this little contribution has many decades of life left in her.

Over time, I've learned for whatever reason that not everyone can say Episcopalian. More than just a few refer to us as Episkopols. Either way, it doesn't matter. Let me be one of the first to welcome you to your spiritual home. I am so thankful that you have chosen to be one of Those Episkopols.

Dennis Maynard, D. Min.
Copyright, © 1987, 1994, 1997, 2002, 2007, 2010
All Rights Reserved
Over One Hundred Thousand Copies in Print

PROLOGUE

"THOSE EPISKOPOLS"

I have been teaching adult inquirer's classes for twenty-five years. My instruction file still resembles my seminary curriculum. My tendency is to walk before the inquirers armed with the details of the four ecumenical councils, the theories of atonement, and the intricacies of the English Reformation. During the question and answer periods, I repeatedly have been brought back to reality. I have been guilty of answering questions the people were not asking. This book is an attempt to answer the questions I repeatedly have been asked by inquirers over the past twenty-five years. There are numerous scholarly works devoted to teaching that which we believe every faithful Episcopalian should know. There is no need for another. I think, however, there is a need to answer the other questions which usually begin with a fascination with "Episkopols".

"Those Episkopols is a factual, humorous, and plain speaking book that will be an invaluable guide to all who are responsible for Inquirer's Class...highest recommendation!"
-The Rev. C. Fredrick Barbee
Editor The Anglican Digest

"...almost thou persuadist me to become an Episcopalian... serious and humorous, with clarity and charity. Father Maynard reveals his devotion to his Anglican heritage while assimilating that heritage in the present."
-G. Avery Lee, M. Div., Litt. D.,
Rector Emeritus, St. Charles Avenue
Baptist Church, New Orleans, Louisiana

"...is a remarkable, readable, and very balanced statement of the Christian faith from the perspective of the Episcopal Church. I am happy to recommend it for congregational use and discussion."
-The Right Reverend Mark Sisk
Bishop
Diocese New York

TABLE OF CONTENTS

Chapter One

WHY ARE THERE
SO MANY DIFFERENT CHURCHES?

On the surface it does look confusing. Just why can't all the denominations get together and be one Church? It was certainly Jesus' final prayer for His Church the night before His crucifixion. He prayed that we all might be one as He and the Father are one.

There is some indication that we might, in fact, be growing closer. Some Baptist churches have put kneelers in their pews, the Methodists occasionally wear vestments and have acolytes, the Presbyterians have robed choirs, the Lutherans wear Roman Collars, the Roman Catholics are having Bible Studies, and some Episcopalians sing Praise Hymns with their hands outstretched like the Pentecostals. At least on the surface, we are beginning to blur some of the differences.

But it is not as simple as all that. It is not just a matter of getting Baptists to baptize their infants, and Methodists to process the cross, and Presbyterians to have Advent wreaths. The differences between the various branches of Christ's Church run deep. The differences are far beneath the differing expressions we see on the surface. While various denominations and congregations can imitate that which they admire in the other, the genetic patterning of each is what really separates us.

I want to present to you three different Pieties I have observed in the Church. These Pieties are the various ways I see Christians living out their experience of God and their journey here on earth. No one piety is the exclusive property of any particular denomination. Some churches borrow freely from each. Individual congregations within a particular denomination may actually adopt a piety that is different from the one predominantly held by their particular denomination.

What must be noted is that each of the pieties I am going to present to you can be argued from scripture. Each has enjoyed popularity at one time or another in the life of the Church. It is these pieties, however, that are the driving force that separates us. It is these pieties that sometimes make it difficult to communicate with one another.

The Good Citizenship Piety

The first piety I want to describe for you is what I call the Good Citizenship Piety. This is a piety that may sound unique to the contemporary American Church. It is not. It is a piety that has historically been utilized during periods of Nationalism whenever the Church could be used as a rallying cry for a particular cause or issue. This is a piety that would equate being a Good Christian with being a Good American. God and Country are closely connected. God, of course, is a white middle class male. A family man with a distinguished record of military service.

This type of piety sees our country as a Christian Nation. Like the Ancient Israelites, we have been chosen by God to point the way for the rest of the world. Quickly, this piety will divide people between the Christians and the pagans. There are the good people and the bad people. There are the God-fearing people and then there are the adulterers, the fornicators, the murderers, the thieves, and the terrorists.

In this type of piety, man is totally depraved and only by the Grace of God can he help himself. Those who have been chosen by God can be found in the Church where they will prove themselves to be among the chosen by keeping all the rules. There is much emphasis in this type of piety on keeping all the rules. Special attention is given to keeping the Puritanical rules of not smoking, drinking, or gambling. In this piety, everyone has an assigned role. You will hear much about what a faithful husband and good father looks like. Women, too, are called to a particular ministry in the

Christian household and are applauded for their deference to men. Children are to follow in the footsteps of their parents and make them proud.

The Church in this piety gathers to "hear a good sermon." There is much emphasis on preaching and the pulpit is central to the life of the Church. This Church is focused on regaining the lost morality of the nation and fighting off all the self-identified enemies of God. Those who are Good Citizens are actively encouraged to join them in their fight. This piety will quickly quote statistics and examples of how the nation and the Church has lost its way. Such a Church seeks to unite America in regaining its lost morality. This lost morality is often focused around a particular political agenda.

One final characteristic of this piety is its emphasis on the will of God. There is a sense in which they believe that everything that happens is God's explicit will. "It is God's will" or "If it is God's will" are common expressions. This piety will try to seek solace in God's will even in the face of great human tragedies or terrible disasters.

The Saved Piety

The second piety I want to discuss is noted for its emphasis on getting people saved. There is an urgency about this since they believe we are living in the last days and Jesus will return at any moment. Only those who have been saved will get to go to heaven. Everyone else will be left here for a terrible time of suffering.

These folks divide the Christian world between those who attend a Bible-preaching Church and those who do not. But even that Church is divided further. Not everyone in the Church is saved, so they divide the Church between those who are merely Church members and those who have been saved.

The Saved Piety has a very definite formula for salvation. A person must do certain things, say certain words, and believe in a certain way, or they will not be able to get the "assurance of salvation and the hope of heaven." A critical question that is often asked by this Saved Piety is, "If you die tonight do you know for a fact that you will be in heaven tomorrow?" If you don't know that in your heart, then you are not yet saved.

Guilt and fear are the two most common tools in this piety's arsenal. There is guilt for having let God down or parents, or spouse, or children, or church, or the preacher. There is fear of going to hell or of being publicly scorned by the Church.

The Church gathers primarily for Bible Study. Members are encouraged to bring their Bibles and the sermon often resembles a long Bible Study Lesson. The worship service is often a very cathartic experience with music that both looks forward to the hope of heaven but also moans the hopelessness of lost sinners.

This particular piety, like the Good Citizenship Piety, has a very definite idea of what a saved person looks like, acts like, and sounds like. There are very clear standards for separating the sheep from the goats. The primary reason for being on this earth is to get other folks saved so that they can go to heaven with them. They offer little hope for people who do not subscribe to their piety and are quite critical of those Churches that do not. After all, they are not saved.

The Sacramental Piety

Obviously the first piety is very past-oriented. There is much emphasis on trying to bring back the good old days. Tremendous energy is put into grieving over that which is lost and trying to recapture the past. "Let's bring back the days when men were men and women were women. Let's bring back the days of patriotism, morality, low crime, the fear of God, full Churches and overflowing offering plates."

The second piety is very future-oriented. This world is an evil place that crucified the very person God sent to save it. "This land is not our home; we are only passing through. We look forward to the day when we can all get to heaven. Then and only then will we know the true joy of God."

The third piety I want to describe for you is very present-oriented. This is a piety that proclaims that the world is a good place. It will tell you that life is good and living is a gift from God. This Church proclaims with Jesus that the Kingdom of God is in our midst. This Church will tell you that God comes to you every day of your life in ten thousand different ways; you need only open your eyes to see Him. This is the predominant piety in the Episcopal Church.

This is a piety that believes that God uses the substance of the universe and the experiences of life to communicate God's love. We believe that the universe itself is sacramental. We believe that Jesus was the greatest sacrament of all. God hallowed flesh and blood in order to be present with us.

This piety believes that we are on a journey. We are on a spiritual journey. We cannot live that journey in isolation so we join together with others on this journey in a common community. We call this community the Church. The Church gathers to receive instruction, to be nourished by the sacraments, and to encourage one another on this journey. The work of the Church is to continue the ministry of Jesus. The Church exists to tell the story of God's love for all people. The Church exists to care for one another, especially those who are ill or in need. The Church exists to serve those who are poor and needy. The Church exists to invite others into a relationship with Jesus and the companionship of the Church on their journey.

Worship in this type of Church is usually an aerobic activity. It is participatory. Worship is something the community does together. The leaders of worship do not see themselves as entertainers but as leaders of the people who are together engaged in the act of worship.

This Church considers all baptized persons to be members of the household of God. This is an inclusive Church that resists classifying or categorizing the faithful. This Church does not see itself as a showcase for saints. Quite to the contrary this is a repentant Church that acknowledges all people to be sinners. This is a church that believes God meets people wherever they are on their spiritual journey. This is a Church that talks of our ongoing need to grow and mature spiritually. This Church does not believe that the work of salvation is completed in this life. This is a Church that prays that the good work we begin here will be continued as we move from strength to strength in the Heavenly Kingdom.

It is this third piety you will read more about in this book. It is a piety that, sadly, separates us from other denominations. It is a piety that sees God's hand at work in the past and rejoices in God's goodness. It is a piety that also believes in the future and celebrates heaven as our destiny. It is, however, a piety that will not mourn the past or hope for the future at the expense of celebrating the goodness of the present. This is a Church that sings, "All Things Bright and Beautiful – All Creatures Great and Small – All Things Wise and Wonderful – The Lord God Made Them All."

Chapter 2

WHY DON'T EPISCOPALIANS
ACT MORE RELIGIOUS?

A few years ago, I had just finished teaching a twelve-week Inquirers' Class for new members and persons wishing to learn more about the Episcopal Church. At the conclusion of the twelfth class I asked the members if they had any reservations, concerns, or questions. A very distinguished woman at the back of the classroom raised her hand. She stated, "For seventy-two years I have been a Christian Scientist. Over the last twelve weeks I have listened to everything that you had to say, and some of it I've heard for the very first time." She continued, "I really do want to become a member of the Episcopal Church, but I think the only way I can become a member of the Episcopal Church is if you will let me be a Scientific Episcopalian."

**When we chose to become Episcopalians,
were we running to embrace something,
or were we running away from something?**

If the truth be known, I should imagine that in the average congregation there are a lot of Scientific Episcopalians. There also are some Baptist Episcopalians, Methodist Episcopalians, Presbyterian Episcopalians, and we even have some Roman Catholic Episcopalians who are just a bit more Catholic than the Pope himself. Some of the statistics suggest that perhaps eighty percent of the members of the Episcopal Church are converts from another denomination. That means that eight out of ten of us grew up in another branch of Christ's Church and at some point in our lives made the decision that we wanted to be Episcopalians.

The critical question I think we have to ask ourselves is this: when we chose to become Episcopalians, were we running to embrace something, or were we running away from something? The answer to that question is very important if we are to understand our own perspective of Anglicanism. If we were, in fact, running to embrace something we felt was missing in our former denomination, then most likely we wanted to bring with us some of that which we were leaving. On occasion we might even get homesick for some of that which we left. If, on the other hand, we were running away from that which we were leaving, then we are likely to resist anything in the Episcopal Church that even slightly resembles that which we left.

In order to understand Anglicanism, in order to understand the Episcopal Church, we have to understand one of the basic tenets of religious life. First comes the faith experience, then comes the theology. First comes the experience of God. Then we reflect on the experience of God, and that becomes our theology. First comes the gospel and the experience of the gospel, then comes the doctrine and the dogma.

The followers of Christ who descend from the British Isles have a unique experience of God. We do not say that we are right and everyone else is wrong. We have a unique theology. We have a unique experience of God that makes us different from others – not right, nor wrong, just unique to us.

In order to get us started, I want to suggest three of the characteristics of Anglicanism. First, we believe God is knowable. We believe that you can know God, you can experience God, you can have a relationship with God. The Apostles' Creed, our baptismal creed, begins, "I believe in" not "I believe that". There is a considerable difference in these two phrases. I can believe that you exist. I can believe that you have a spouse, a job, children. I can even believe you are a person of considerable worth, but that does not mean that I believe in you. It does not mean that I trust you, that I love you, or that I have a relationship with you. We Anglicans say that we believe in God. We can have a relationship with God now. God is knowable. We can trust God. We can love God. We can relate to God.

The second thing I want to suggest is that we believe creation is good. The world is good! We do not believe that this is an evil place. After God created each element of creation, God said, "It is good". To know creation is to know God. I believe it was Madeline L'Engle who said, "Heaven is not good because the world is bad." Jesus said, "The kingdom of God is in your midst." Here, now, we can be a part of it. When we sing our hymns in the Episcopal Church, we do not sing about a sinful and evil world. We sing about the glory of God's creation. We sing, "All things bright and beautiful, the Lord God made them all." And so we affirm that creation is good.

The third characteristic I would suggest is that we Anglicans embrace all of life. We think life is to be celebrated, that life and living are good and happy things. Through the years we Episcopalians have suffered a lot of silly abuse about our attitudes towards drinking, dancing, playing cards, and admiring the human anatomy. While we think it is silly, it is the consequence of refusing to divide the world into the physical and the spiritual. We resist anything that resembles dualism. We do not believe salvation lies in avoiding the material and concentrating on the spiritual. We Anglicans know that overcoming sin is not quite as easy as living a spartan life.

In the movie *The Gods Must Be Crazy*, an airline pilot is seen flying over a remote part of Africa. He is drinking Coca-Cola from a bottle. He decides at one point to throw the Coca-Cola bottle out the window. He does, and the bottle descends from the heavens and falls very near a family of bushmen. The bushmen see the bottle coming and decide since it came from the heavens it must be a gift from God. They never have seen a Coca-Cola bottle before. They take it back to their village. They admire it and reflect on why the gods must have given it to them. They've had the experience. Now they begin to formulate their theology about this Coca-Cola bottle. They decide, in fact, the gods want them to have it and it is a wonderful thing. So they begin to use it as a tool. They even blow into it and make music out of it. The gods have given them a wondrous gift. But then the dark side of human nature begins to manifest itself. The Coca-Cola bottle becomes for them an evil thing. The bottle becomes an object of envy. People resent those who are using it when they don't have it. It becomes an object of anger and eventually becomes a weapon. They decide that to rid themselves of these sins they must get rid of the bottle. One of them takes it upon himself to walk to the end of the world and throw the bottle off the edge of the earth. The gods must take their gift back.

The bottle was not evil. Nor do we believe that God's world is evil. It's how we respond to God's world that makes something evil or good. We Anglicans believe that God can communicate his love and his grace to us through the physical and that to know God's creation is to know God. In the Episcopal Church we do not bless things in order to make them holy. We bless God who has given us all good things. There is a big difference.

Episcopalians make a distinction between religion and the spiritual life. Religion tends to compartmentalize life. There is the religious part where one does religious things and tries to sound religious. Religion is about keeping up an image. Religious people are quite concerned that other people perceive them to be religious. Religion is concerned about doctrines and dogmas and arguing over who is right, who is wrong, who is saved, and who is damned. We believe living the spiritual life is about inquiry.

Episcopalians do not believe that we can divide our lives into the religious or "church" portion, and our secular life. We believe God is in all that we do and that living the spiritual life is a twenty-four hour affair. We have tried to avoid the hypocrisy that blesses behavior in one aspect of our lives, but would condemn it as inappropriate when we are gathered to be "churchy". We believe we are the church individually and corporately wherever we are and whatever we are doing. We cannot remove our Christianity simply by taking off our Sunday Clothing.

Episcopalians in America are a part of a much larger communion of Christians known as the Anglican Communion. It is a worldwide communion with the Archbishop of Canterbury as the titular head. This worldwide fellowship is drawn together by certain common marks. The first is that because we are a worldwide Church we try to take a global view of things. We cannot be parochial and isolationist. We must consider the impact of our decisions on people far removed from us.

Second, we celebrate our diversity. Tolerance is not an excuse or a sign of weakness, but it is our strength. We have not traded tolerance for Truth, but we value tolerance as an essential ingredient in each person's pursuit of Truth.

Third, we are a noncompetitive people. We do not feel the need to push our beliefs on others. We do not believe that everyone should be an Episcopalian. We reject knee-in-the-chest evangelism. Ours is a "seeker-friendly" church where we believe God will meet us wherever we are on our spiritual journey. Salvation, for us, is the journey. It is not a merit badge to wear.

Fourth, we are idealists. We take words like peacemaker, mercy, grace, equality, and so forth seriously. We strive to incarnate those words into this universe. We believe in living into the ideals of Jesus and forgiving ourselves and others when we fail to do so. We strive for perfection while living daily with the discontent of our imperfections.

Fifth, we are content to live with questions. We do not believe that we have to have an answer for everything. There are many mysteries of the universe we will never fully comprehend, nor is it intended that we do so. We have an intense respect for thoughtful holiness. We resist giving people simple answers to complex questions. One only wonders how many people have been turned off to Christianity because they were given simplistic answers. Anglicans value the work of the Spirit in medicine, science, and all the academic disciplines. We do not see ourselves in opposition to any field of inquiry, but in concert with it.

Sixth, we believe that the spiritual journey is a communal activity. When we invite a person to walk in the way of Jesus, we are asking them to do so in a company of other travelers. The people of God that we call the Church are here to strengthen and encourage one another in our spiritual life. We do this when we come together for our common act of worship and learning. We do this when we care for one another in the good times and the bad with our ministries of presence, prayer, and kindness. We do this when we work together to alleviate the suffering of those who are oppressed in mind, body, or spirit. And we do this when we invite others to join us on our journey. When we come together as the Church in large groups or small, we are strengthened and encouraged by God and by one another.

I began by saying that the purpose of this book is not to suggest in any way that we are right and everyone else is wrong, but simply to reaffirm what we as Anglicans believe. I'd like to illustrate that for you. Think of the Christian faith, if you will, as a great symphony orchestra in which there are many sections. There are the flutes, the brass, the woodwinds, the strings, and the timpani. Each section of the orchestra has its part to play in order for the symphony to be heard in all of its fullness. No one part can pretend to be the entire orchestra. Nor can the symphony be heard in its fullness if one part insists on drowning out the other parts, or if one part thinks it is the only part that should be heard. We Anglicans have our part. It is important for us to play it, and it is important for us to play it boldly. While we recognize that our part is not the right part for everyone, it is the right part for us. We are called to faithfully play our part. It's up to God to use our message and to use us as He chooses.

Chapter 3

CAN YOU GET SAVED IN THE EPISCOPAL CHURCH?

One of my favorite stories on the Episcopal Church is about the man who, in the contemporary jargon, had become a new Christian. He was quite enthusiastic about his faith and one day decided to visit the Episcopal Church. He participated in the worship service with a tremendous amount of gusto. When the Rector preached his sermon, the man began to periodically interrupt the Rector's preaching with words of acclamation. He would shout, "Alleluia" or "Praise the Lord" or "Amen". As you can imagine, this was very distracting to the rest of the Episcopal congregation. One of the ushers went to where the man was seated and whispered in the man's ear, "Fellow, you have to be quiet in here." The gentleman said, "Oh, it's okay. I've just got religion." The usher would not be deterred. "Now listen. This is the Episcopal Church. You have to be quiet in here. If you got religion, you didn't get it here!"

Through the years, we Episcopalians have taken a lot of ridicule over the way we approach the business of salvation and the work of our church. We've been labeled everything from "The Republican Party at Prayer" to "The Country Club with the Cross on Top" to "The Frozen Chosen."

One summer, my wife Nancy and I were at the beach. We met another couple on the beach and were getting acquainted. They did not know what I do for a living, but they knew we were from Greenville, South Carolina. As you often will do when you meet someone for the first time, we asked, "Who do you know from Greenville?" We found out there was someone we both knew. So Nancy said to them, "Did you realize that person is studying for the priesthood?" The man protested, "A preacher? That person wants to be a preacher?" His wife tried to calm him. "Now, dear, he's going to be an Episcopal priest – Episcopal priest, that's not quite as bad."

A few years ago *Playboy* magazine did us a really big favor. They named the Episcopal priesthood as one of the best jobs you can get. Now the insinuation in all of that is that we Episcopalians really don't take our religion all that seriously.

Salvation is the work of Jesus and so it is the work of His church, all branches of His church, including the Episcopal Church. What we often object to is how that work is described and what is intended. The question often is phrased this way, "Are you saved?" What is intended is to discern whether or not you have at some point in your life held your hand up at a prayer meeting and said that you accept Jesus Christ as your Lord and Savior. Or, at a revival meeting have you ever responded to the altar call and gone forward to kneel at a mourners' bench. While there, you are to pray to the point that you receive a warm feeling that would assure you that you have, in fact, been saved.

If we stray, we stray as a prodigal son or prodigal daughter of God. If we return, we return through repentance and not through baptism.

That question, and all that is intended along with that question, is not a part of our Anglican heritage. It is not a part of our tradition. In fact it is much more a part of eighteenth century revivalism. Eighteenth century revivalism taught that in the salvation process you could receive what is called the consolation. The consolation is that at some point you could pray until you got a warm glow. That warm feeling assured you that you had been saved. Seeking some sort of emotional experience is outside the Anglican tradition. We believe that the assurance of our salvation is far too critical to be left to anything so elusive as our feelings. Such emotionalism is out of our heritage. We don't run around asking one another, "Are you saved?"

We Anglicans really reject the "Are you saved?" mentality for two reasons. The first is that the "I am saved" attitude suggests that there is no room for improvement. Somehow or another the saved already have locked up the whole salvation process. It is finished. Perfection has been achieved.

The second reason we reject that particular phraseology is that as Anglicans we believe that salvation is a process. In that process one must change and grow and mature. I want to suggest to you four characteristics of salvation as we Anglicans understand it.

The first is that we believe that the salvation process begins with baptism. The chief of the Apostles, Peter, wrote in his Epistle, "Baptism is not the washing away of bodily pollution, but it is the appeal made to God and it (baptism) brings salvation through the resurrection of Jesus Christ." Our Prayer Book directs the priest to bless the water before baptism and in reciting the blessing over the water the priest recalls that through baptism we are reborn or in today's jargon, "born again". We are reborn by the Holy Spirit. In the Anglican Church, in the Episcopal Church, there is no mourners' bench but there is a baptismal font. We believe that the Christian journey begins with baptism. It is the rite of initiation. It is when one becomes a Christian. It is when one becomes a member of the church and one becomes a Christian in the truest sense of the word. In the old covenant, one became a Jew when the male was circumcised, so today we become Christians when we are baptized. Baptism is the mark of the Christian. It is through baptism that we are sealed and marked as Christ's own forever. It is through the waters of baptism that God assures us of our salvation, not through our feelings. If we then stray away, we stray as a prodigal son or prodigal daughter of God. If we are to return to God, we return through repentance and not (through baptism) by being baptized again.

The second characteristic of the salvation process, as we Anglicans hold it, is that we are nurtured by the Holy Eucharist. It is to be nurtured by the sacrament of Holy Communion. When I was a child they used to advertise Wonder Bread. They said Wonder Bread builds bodies in twelve different ways. Well, the Holy

Eucharist builds strong Christians. It is the food of the Anglican sojourner. You know, it's hard for us to estimate the totality, even the centrality, of the Holy Eucharist for Christians over the past two thousand years because it has just always been there. Consider the centrality of the Eucharist in our lives. In the context of the Holy Eucharist, we baptize our children, we confirm our new members, we ordain our clergy. People are married and people are buried in the context of the Holy Communion. In the context of Holy Communion our churches are consecrated, our priests are instituted, and our lay ministers are commissioned. In the context of Holy Communion the scriptures are read, the gospel is proclaimed, our sins are forgiven. We lay hands on the sick. We pray for the church, the world, and ourselves. It's through these sacred mysteries of the bread and the wine that we gather week after week as Christians and we pray, "Lord Jesus, be known to us as you were to your disciples in the breaking of the bread."

The third characteristic of the salvation process as we Anglicans understand it is that it requires that we change and grow and mature. It is an ongoing process. A few weeks ago someone said to me, "Boy, I heard the most wonderful sermon (at another church they had visited). In fact, it was the best sermon I'd ever heard in my entire life." I said, "Gosh, I'd like to have heard that sermon. What made it so good?" This person replied, "There wasn't a dry eye in the house. Everyone in that entire congregation cried." "That's what made it a good sermon – everybody cried?" He said, "Yes." I've heard some sermons that made me want to cry, but not for those reasons. In the Episcopal Church, the point of the sermon is not to dredge up all kinds of sentimentalism within us in order to make us all goose pimply. It's not to get us stirred up so that we will make an emotional commitment to some cause. Our clergy are trained to preach for insight and for understanding. We are to take that insight and understanding and empty ourselves in such a way that Christ might be able to fill us.

I was teaching a confirmation course a few years ago. One of the inquirers accused, "Well, you Episcopalians never have an altar call." I responded, "You're wrong. We have an altar call every Sunday. Every Sunday there is an altar call in the Episcopal Church." Have you not ever heard these words, "Ye who do truly and earnestly repent you of your sins, and are in love and charity with your neighbors, and intend to lead a new life, following the commandments of God, and walking from henceforth in his holy ways: Draw near with faith, and make your humble confession to Almighty God, devoutly kneeling." Now, is that not an altar call? Does that not call us to reexamine our lives? Does that not call us to get in good charity with our neighbors and with God and make reconciliation with those from whom we are alienated? Does that not call us to re-examine our life and make a new intention to follow God in a new way, or in today's jargon, recommit ourselves to Jesus Christ? You see, recommitment, repentance, making a decision for God is an ongoing process. We make it every Sunday, and hopefully we make it every day as we commit ourselves anew.

Episcopalians have an altar call every Sunday.

When we come to the communion rail I suggest this devotion. As you raise your hands to receive the bread, pray, "Out with self. Out with Dennis. Out with envy. Out with anger. Out with greed." Then take the host in your hands and pray, "In with Jesus. In with compassion. In with forgiveness. In with understanding. In with love." Sunday by Sunday, day by day, as we go through that process, hopefully we will be able to say along with Saint Paul, "It is not I, but Christ who is within me."

It's really important for us to understand that we're not called to be Christians. We're called to be Christ. There is a difference between the Anglican approach to salvation and the revivalistic approach to salvation. That difference is similar to being placed in a nice warm oven and being baked very slowly at a low temperature, versus being stir-fried. Think about it.

The fourth thing I'd like to suggest to you is that the process of salvation as we Anglicans understand it requires that we be honest. We must be honest with ourselves, we must be honest with one another, and we must be honest with our God. There is no room for playing games. A fellow was caught stealing chickens. He was taken before the judge and the judge asked him, "Are you the defendant?" He answered, "No, your honor, I'm the guy who stole the chickens." In the salvation process, it is very important for us to be honest.

Repentance is a very important part of the spiritual journey for Anglicans. To acknowledge our sins, confess our sins, make restitution where possible, and amend our lives in order to avoid being tempted again. These are the four steps of repentance. Confessing our sins to a priest is known as the Sacrament of Reconciliation. This is an opportunity given to Episcopalians. It is not required. Hearing ourselves confess our sins, receiving the benefit of counsel, and being assured of forgiveness are of tremendous aid to those who would learn from their errors.

Sadly, even in the Episcopal Church there are those clergy and lay people who have a very narrow definition of salvation. There are those who delight in dividing the Body of Christ into two groups – Episcopalians and those who are Born Again. The Born Again are those who have publicly walked the aisle or signed a commitment card at an Evangelistic Rally. The Born Again will tell you that it was on that occasion that they "accepted the Lord and became a Christian". Sadly, they will tell the rest of us that we are not real Christians and that if we die tonight we will not go to heaven. They will tell us that unless we follow certain steps outlined for us in one of the pamphlets they carry with them, invite Jesus into our hearts in their presence, or some other initiation rite, then we are only Episcopalians, and we are not saved, nor are we Christians.

The following lines are attributed to an English Church leaflet. They may best summarize our Anglican view of those who think they have a corner on the salvation market and the inside track on who is going to be in heaven.

Take These Lines to Heart

I dreamed death came to me one night
and heaven's gates flew open wide.
With kindly grace St. Peter came and
ushered me inside.
There to my astonishment were friends
I had known on earth,
Some I had labeled as unfit and some
of little worth.
Indignant words flew to my lips:
Words I could not set free,
For every face showed stunned surprise –
No one expected me.

The Episcopal Church, like every church, has those who will narrowly define what it is to be a Christian. If you don't read the Bible a certain way, pray a certain way, or worship in a certain manner, then you are not a real Christian. Such narrow definitions of Christianity are far outside the Catholic Faith as we Anglicans understand it. They are not in keeping with the faith delivered to the apostles. Of course, we are not opposed to having folks invite Jesus into their hearts, or read pamphlets, or pray as the Spirit leads them. We are only opposed to those who would have us believe they have a corner on the God market and all of the rest of us must have the same experience of God as they have had. We welcome all experiences of God and reject none of the gifts of God or none of the wondrous methods God uses to bring people into relationship with the Almighty. Anglicans do resist those who would have us believe that we all must have the same gift and the same experience. We resist those who would tell us we have to read scripture their way, pray their way, and worship their way. We resist those messages even when they are coming from people inside the Episcopal Church. We value their ministries among us, but remind them that it is God who designs the plan of salvation for each of us and not we humans. The Episcopal Church welcomes all people regardless of where they are on their spiritual journey and regardless of their unique experience of God. We resist dividing people into merit groups. All baptized persons are Christians. All members are sinners, even those who will tell us that they have been born again.

I once had someone say to me, "I'm not going to go to church because it's just filled with hypocrites." I asked, "Where are the hypocrites supposed to go?" The church is the perfect place for hypocrites. It's like saying that one is not going to go to the hospital because it's filled with sick people. The church is a hospital for the sick. It's a hospital for sinners. We Anglicans do not believe that the church is a haven for saints. We do not believe that it is a club for the elite. We do not believe that it is the hideout for the saved. The church is the gathering place for wounded healers. The church exists for those people in this life who have been injured by their own sins and the sins of others. Here in the presence of Jesus we can reach out and touch one another. Here, we can touch Him, and we can be made whole.

Recently I told someone that there is a sense in which the Episcopal Church exists for those people who don't think they're good enough to belong to any other church. If you have a problem with that, consider the church that Jesus gathered around himself. Consider those who were in the inner circle of Jesus' congregation. They were the people whose sins were so public that there was absolutely no way they could hide them. In His presence they sought to become new creations.

Here is a prayer attributed to a Negro slave that summarizes the Anglican approach to salvation:

> Lord, I know that I'm not all that I ought to be;
> And I know that I am not yet all that I'm gonna be;
> But Lord, I sure thank you I'm not what I used to be.

If you understand that prayer, then you understand the Anglican approach to salvation.

Chapter 4

CAN YOU BELIEVE ANYTHING YOU WANT AND BE AN EPISCOPALIAN?

There are diverse opinions in the Episcopal Church. Some Episcopalians prefer Elizabethan language, others contemporary.

Anglicans value their freedom.
We do not want to be
A part of a church that tells us...

Some Episcopalians prefer Bach, others renewal music. This list of preferences is incredible, ranging from incense to women bishops and priests. Further, the Episcopal Church allows issues to come before its convention that more conservative churches would never allow on the agenda. Anglicans value their freedom. We do not want to be a part of a church that tells us what books we can and cannot read, what questions we can and cannot ask. There are no imprimaturs, no book bans, no gag orders. There is freedom, openness, and dialogue. From time to time this freedom makes us uncomfortable, but we prefer it. Autocratic rules produce clones. Freedom produces diversity. This diversity is housed under one roof. It is the natural by-product of the way we do our theology. It is critical to our pursuit of truth.

First, Anglican belief rests on a three-legged stool – scripture, tradition, and reason. We try to keep all three of them in balance. We begin with the primacy of scripture. We say that the scriptures contain all things necessary for salvation. We say that the scriptures should be the primary emphasis of our church and therefore should be taught at all levels. Having said that, we then say that while the scriptures contain all things necessary for salvation, they do not contain all things. The scriptures should be taught, but they are not the only things that should be taught. The scriptures have to be interpreted, and they have to be interpreted in light of tradition and in light of reason. We Anglicans are mindful of the fact that the three Persons of the Holy Trinity are not "Holy Father, Holy Son, and Holy Scripture".

When we study the Bible we ask who wrote the particular passage, to whom they were writing, what the situation was at the time, why they wrote it. We try to understand it in light of all those questions. The scriptures have to be interpreted in light of tradition. My definition of tradition is this: tradition is the record of Christians through the centuries, both understanding and misunderstanding God. Because we misunderstand God on occasion, it's very important that we bring the third ingredient, reason, to the theological process. We believe as Anglicans that God is still speaking to us. We do not believe that the scriptures were closed and God said, "That's it. You're on your own now. I'm not ever going to talk to you again. Everything you need to know is in the book." We don't believe that at the close of the great Ecumenical Councils, God simply turned his back on us and said, "All right, gang, you're on your own now. I'm not ever going to talk to you again." We believe that God still talks to us through reason, intuitive reasoning and factual reasoning. God still speaks to us through the intuitive reasoning of the artist and the poet and the musician. God still speaks to us through the factual reasoning of the scientist, the sociologist, psychology, and psychiatry. We believe that all seeking leads to God, for all knowledge comes from God and all knowledge will take us back to God. The Anglican Church is a very spiritual church. We place great emphasis on the three Persons of the Holy Trinity as "Holy Father, Holy Son, Holy Spirit".

The Episcopal Church has been called the thinking person's church

The second thing that I think contributes to the diversity is that we are not a dogmatic church. We like to believe that Jesus is central to our church, and not dogmas. At the Protestant Reformation, we did not become a confessional church. We did not adopt a series of dogmas that you have to believe in order to be a good Episcopalian. That doesn't mean that we're a church without teachings. We have teachings. We have the Bible. We have our Book of Common Prayer. We have our hymnal. We have the Godly Admonitions of our Bishops and we have the decisions of our church councils. Overall we have been content to say that the Apostles' Creed, the baptismal creed, is a sufficient statement for those who want to be baptized in this church and that the Nicene Creed is a sufficient statement of what we believe. We have resisted becoming a dogmatic church for good reason. First, dogmas can become a wall to the ongoing revelations of God. The Episcopal Church has been called the thinking person's religion. It's the thinking person's religion because we encourage people to think. We don't see the asking of questions as being an evil thing but we see questions as good. Questions are healthy. We do not see that having faith doubts is the same as having a lack of faith. We all have doubts from time to time – be careful not to deny that. Such doubts are a normal part of the faith process and thereby are good and healthy. The opposite of faith is not doubt, but fear.

We resist dogmas for another reason. We think they obstruct spiritual growth. The very place that we dig in our heels, the very place we decide we're going to be inflexible, rigid, obstinate, even stubborn – that may be the very place God is calling us to grow and mature. Convictions are not necessarily the equivalent of faith. From time to time we need to examine our rigid convictions in light of this question – of what are we afraid? The answer to that question might give us a lot of insight into ourselves and our faith. A lack of tolerance may not be faith but fear, a fear we need to deal with.

We resist dogmas because dogmas are designed to defend a God who needs no defending. God will be God whether defended or not. What happens is that we very often end up with a dogma that is itself defenseless. When the Pope visited South America, he appeared before a very poor farm village. The people were living in dirt shacks. The average income was $300 a year. The people had twelve, thirteen, fourteen and fifteen children. The Pope had to defend the dogma against birth control which is based on a pre-scientific understanding of reproduction. Dogmas often end up being defenseless.

We resist dogmas, finally, because they can lead to prejudice. If you don't agree with my conviction, if you don't agree with my dogmas, it is but a brief step to conclude, "You are wrong and because you are wrong, then you are not a Christian and because you are not a Christian, then you are the enemy and someone to be discriminated against." For the Anglican, given a choice between heresy and schism, we see schism as the greater sin. We do not seek to learn more of God's truth so that we can use these new insights as weapons against unbelievers or those who believe differently. We value reason and learning so that we can come closer to Truth for Truth's sake because we believe God is Truth.

A Jewish visitor from Israel once went to our great cathedral in New York City, St. John the Divine. He remarked to the person showing him around, "All religions reject, reject, reject, exclude, exclude, exclude, but I come to your Anglican Cathedral and what do I find? In statuary and glass I find labor and management side by side. I find athletics and psychiatry side by side." And so it is in our Anglican cathedrals – there is Athanasius and Augustine and Acquinas, but there is also Luther and Calvin and Wesley. There are artists and poets and authors, but there is science, medicine, and religion. Anglicans do not exclude, but Anglicans include, include, include because we believe all knowledge comes from God and will ultimately lead us back to God.

There is a concerted effort in the Anglican Communion to make sure our faith is both comprehensive and inclusive. There is respect for differing points of view. Respecting a differing view provides us an opportunity to examine our own view and to learn from others. Overall, we choose to focus on those things that unite us and not focus on those things that divide us.

The final reason I think our Church produces diversity is the very nature of our understanding of the Christian faith. The Anglican understanding of faith breeds diversity within our church. We define faith as a relationship with God. The church does not exist to tell people what to believe. The church exists to manifest in whom they are to believe. Our task is to create worshiping communities in which people can know God and make God known. This faith is a relationship with God. Faith is an attitude of trust with God or to paraphrase the definition that's in the Book of Hebrews, "Faith is believing and acting as though everything we hope is true, is true."

I've often thought on the question that the resurrected Christ asked Simon Peter. He asked him the question three times. He said, "Peter, do you love me? Peter, do you love me?" I think on the day of judgment that's the question that Jesus is going to ask us. He's not going to ask, "Did you get all my dogmas correct? Did you convince everybody of the right theology? Did you get them to interpret the scriptures the right way? Did you win every argument? Did you prove to the world that you were right and everybody else was wrong?" I don't think those are the questions Jesus will ask us. I think he's going to say to us one by one, "Do you love me? Did you love my brothers and sisters? Did you feed my sheep?"

Here is my description of the Anglican Communion:

If you're looking for a church that has
Morality but not moralism,
The Bible but not bibliolatry,
Law but not legalism,
Emotion but not emotionalism.
Piety but not pietism,
Tradition but not sentimentalism,
Then you're probably in the right place.

If you're looking for a church where diversity is
celebrated and not condemned,
where thinking is stimulated and not discouraged,
where righteous living is of greater value
than right talking,
where being loving is more important than being right,
you're in the right place.

If you're looking for a church where Jesus is central,
a church that is not afraid to ask difficult questions of Him and of
itself,
then you are in the right place.

But one word of caution.
in such a church open to the ongoing revelations of God
people will constantly be required
to look at old things in new ways.

Chapter 5

WHY DO EPISCOPALIANS READ THEIR PRAYERS?

When one of our former Presiding Bishops, John Hines, was living in Houston, Texas, one weekend he and his wife entertained the Bishop of Johannesburg and his spouse, Bishop and Mrs. Ambrose Reeves. They decided that on Saturday they would introduce them to the American custom of football. Bishop and Mrs. Hines took Bishop and Mrs. Reeves to a Rice University football game. On this particular Saturday, Rice University was playing Texas Christian University. Texas Christian University had a slight edge on the scoreboard and was quite literally pushing Rice University all over the field. Bishop and Mrs. Hines realized early on that it would be too formidable a task to explain American football to people who had never before seen an American football game. So they were content just to sit back and answer the questions that Bishop and Mrs. Reeves might have. Each time Texas Christian University would come close to scoring against Rice University, all of the Rice freshman were compelled to come out of the stands, go into the threatened end zone, and there kneel before the school's mascot, a great stuffed owl. There they were to pray that Texas Christian University would not score against them. Well, this most certainly got Mrs. Reeves and the Bishop's attention. So Mrs. Reeves asked Mrs. Hines, "What on earth are they doing?" Mrs. Hines responded, "Oh, they're praying to their owl that he will prevent Texas Christian University from scoring against them, "to which Mrs. Reeves exclaimed, "Oh my goodness. The Christians are winning and they're not even praying."

To even the most casual observer it would appear that on occasion the people who are not praying in this world are the ones who are doing the winning. So it is only right that we ask ourselves, "Does it do any good to pray?" Having asked the question, we note that at the very heart of religious people is prayer. It is the one thing that we hold in common with all religions. All religious people pray. At the heart of being a Christian is the act of prayer and at the very core of what it is to be an Anglican or to be Episcopalian is the act of prayer.

The Book of Common Prayer is central to the life of the Episcopalian. In this book are prayers for every transitional moment in our life from birth until death and beyond. In this book are prayers to offer at the beginning of the day and at the end of the day. Because this prayer book is so central to the life of an Episcopalian, since it plays such a vital role in who we are and how we go about living out our spiritual journey, we Episcopalians often have been accused of not knowing how to pray. It has been said that we have to read our prayers, that we really don't know how to pray. It reminds me of the time that one of the lay women in the parish I served in Dallas was called to a planning meeting for the World Day of Prayer Service that was going to be held in that city. All of the women came together to plan this ecumenical service that would celebrate their life of prayer together. My Episcopal lay woman was very enthused about this and made a great many contributions to the discussions. They decided that they would end their planning meeting with a prayer. They called on my Episcopal lay woman to pray. She went into an absolute panic. She glanced all around the room but there was no prayer book in sight. The only words that would come to her mind were "Now I lay me down to sleep." We know the accusation that Episcopalians don't know how to pray isn't true, but what we need to understand is what we mean by prayer and how we go about our life of prayer. We have to begin with the Prayer Book. There are seven things I'd like to suggest to you that we can learn about prayer in the Episcopal Church as substantiated in the Book of Common Prayer.

The Book of Common Prayer protects us from one another's creativity, bad theology and current passion.

The first thing we need to understand is that every revision of the Book of Common Prayer has been based upon a critical premise in Anglicanism, *Lex orandi, lex credendi – Lex credendi, lex orandi*. Translated, "The law of prayer is the law of faith. The law of faith is the law of prayer, "or even more succinctly, "What we pray is what we believe, and what we believe is what we pray." When we come together for common prayer we are dependent upon this book. It contains the wisdom of the ages. Some of these prayers are thousands of years of age. Some of them were familiar to the lips of Jesus. These prayers are most appropriate for public worship because these are the prayers that we have all agreed on. We hold these things in common. When we pray these things we know we all believe them. We all believe them so therefore we can pray them. That's not always the case with extemporaneous prayer; you might offer in your prayer sentiments with which I would not necessarily agree. In fact, you might offer sentiments that no one else would agree with. More often than not what you might offer would be a sermon preached with our eyes shut. So we believe that when we come together for common worship we should offer those prayers which we have all commonly agreed to. Basically, the Book of Common Prayer protects us from one another's creativity or lack thereof. It protects us from one another's bad theology, and it protects us from one another's current passion.

The second characteristic of prayer in the Anglican life that we can learn from the Book of Common Prayer is that these prayers become a fabric of our spiritual journey. They become a part of who we are as Christians. One of the things that I've tried to do since going to an Episcopal seminary is to make a morning offering. A morning offering is a short prayer that one might offer first thing in the morning when one regains consciousness. One can adjust one's attitude toward God and one's responsibilities for the day. I've not had a great deal of success with morning offerings. There are many mornings when I really didn't want to say good morning to God. I really wanted to say, "Good God, it's morning!" A few years ago I happened upon a collect in the Book of Common Prayer in the service of Morning Prayer. I try to remember to offer this collect each morning.

O Lord, our Heavenly Father, Almighty Everlasting
God, You have brought us safely to the beginning of
this day. Defend us in the same with your mighty
power and grant that this day we fall into no sin, nor
run into any kind of danger, but that we being ordered
by your governance may do always what is righteous
in your sight.

That's just hard to improve upon. Is this not an appropriate way to begin each day? There's another prayer that's not in our prayer book but is attributed to a theologian by the name of Reinhold Niebuhr. Niebuhr's prayer has come to be called The Serenity Prayer. It's very much a part of my spiritual journey. It is invaluable to me when facing stress and confusion.

God, grant me the serenity to accept those things I
cannot change, the courage to change those things I
can, and the wisdom to know the difference.

Such a prayer becomes a part of the fabric of one's life. It is hard for me to describe completely for you what happens when clergy go to the hospital to see someone who is anxious about surgery, anxious about medical tests, or near death. It is hard for me to do justice to the experience of opening the Prayer Book and praying for the ill the prayers that they've heard their entire life. The prayers bring comfort. The peace of God which passes understanding pours over them.

The third thing we Anglicans believe about prayer is that we try never to get ourselves in a situation of saying either/or. Either you have written prayers or you have extemporaneous prayers. We believe both/and. You do both. You have written prayer and you have extemporaneous prayers. There's a time in all of our prayer lives to simply open ourselves to God and to pour our hearts out to the Almighty in our own words. But the most important thing that we've got to keep in mind about extemporaneous praying is this – it is not necessary for us to get goose pimply. It is not necessary for us to cry. It is not necessary for us to feel anything in order for God to hear our prayers. That doesn't mean you can't have the good feelings of forgiveness and thanksgiving and comfort and solace that can come to us when we pray. Prayer can produce those feelings. But God hears us even when we don't feel anything at all. God hears us!

The fourth thing that I would like to suggest to you about prayer is that prayer is an act of love. It is a way that we can show one another and our God that we love them. It's one of the reasons we still pray for people who have departed this life. We loved them when they were in this life and we prayed for them when they were in this life. Just because they have departed this life doesn't mean we should stop praying for them. Someone once defined prayer as loving your neighbor on your knees.

The fifth thing I'd like to suggest to you is that prayer unleashes the powers of faith. Prayer is a means of communication with God. It is a means whereby we can build and strengthen our trust, dependence and openness to God. In this life it's a lot easier for us to listen to somebody tell us "no" when we know that they love us. Whether it's parents or a spouse or a person in authority, we can accept that "no" much more easily if we know that they love us and care for us and they only want the very best for us. It is also true of God. We can accept both the "yes" and "no" of our prayer lives a lot better if we know that we believe in a God who wants only the very best for us.

The sixth thing I'd like to suggest to you is that prayer requires that we discern our responsibilities in life. We have to discern that which is our responsibility and that which is God's. I've known people who prayed that they might receive a healing, but yet their hearts were filled with anger, hatred, bitterness, and a lack of forgiveness for someone else. Our Prayer Book teaches us that if we are to pray for healing it must be a total healing, not just of the body but of the mind and the spirit as well. When we pray for a miracle, it is important for us to discern whether or not we have done our part. Have we done all that we can to make the miracle possible? And when we pray for peace in the world it is important for us to recognize that peace begins with us. When we petition God for ourselves or others, it is important for us us to discern whether or not we are asking God to do something for us that we really are supposed to do for ourselves. I once heard someone say, "Prayer changes things." The thing that very often is changed is us.

The last thing that I'd like to suggest to you about prayer is that prayer is not something we talk about. Prayer is something one does. In the decades from the 1930's through the 1960's, Yale Divinity School was quite literally dominated by H. Richard Niebuhr. Richard was the brother of Reinhold who is attributed with writing The Serenity Prayer. Niebuhr had an incredibly brilliant mind, but he also was a man of prayer. He prayed all the time. He prayed before each meal. He would pray before each class session. He would pray when a student came to visit him. It was said that you could see Niebuhr walking across the campus and he would just stop where he was and start praying out loud in front of everyone else. However, his prayers were very childlike, very simple, not at all representative of the great theological mind we associate with Niebuhr's works. The students decided that one of them was going to have to go ask Niebuhr about his theology of prayer. So lots were cast and the lot fell on one particular student. The student went to Dr. Niebuhr and said, "Dr. Niebuhr, what is your theology of prayer? Your prayers are so childlike. You pray so simply. You pray as though God is standing right next to you. What is your theology of prayer?" Dr. Niebuhr responded, "I have no theology of prayer. Prayer is not something you talk about. Prayer is something you do." (Prayer is not something to talk about. Prayer is something to do.)

The Book of Common Prayer is central to what it is to be an Anglican. The overwhelming majority of the words in the Book of Common Prayer are words of scripture. It is the Bible put into prayer. The Book of Common Prayer is not designed for us to discuss. It's designed for us to use. If we are to understand the life of prayer for an Episcopalian, we have to become familiar with the Prayer Book because in that book are prayers for our own needs and the needs of others. We won't find any prayers for our wants. We will find prayers for our needs. We will find prayers for doctors and nurses that they might be instruments of healing. We'll find prayers for miracles, those that we cannot understand and those that occur every day that we do understand and take for granted. Prayer is not something we talk about. Prayer is something that we are to do. When we look in the Prayer Book we should keep in mind that what we pray is what we believe and what we believe is what we pray. The Book of Common Prayer is the work of a people who believe strongly in the power of prayer. Episcopalians believe that prayer can change us, prayer can change the life of the people we love and care for, prayer can even change the circumstances of the universe in which we live.

Chapter 6

DOES GOD LIKE ALL THAT RITUAL?

One of the best remembered and sometimes requested stories that I tell is about the inebriated man who happened into the Episcopal Church one Sunday morning. He had never before been to an Episcopal Church so he was somewhat taken back by the building itself. Soon the great procession began. In came the acolytes carrying the cross and torches, followed by a large choir wearing robes. The inebriated man looked askance at that. He'd never seen anything like that before in his life. A few seconds later, along came another cross and more torches. Then came all the acolytes wearing their robes. Well, this was almost too much for him. Then came yet another cross and the clergy dressed in all their various and sundry gowns and vestments. The inebriated man was sure he was in the wrong place. He almost had all he could handle. Just then the Bishop entered. The Bishop was wearing his big hat, his mitre. He had on his gold cope and was carrying an incense pot. He was swinging the incense pot as he went along. The inebriated man had now had his fill. He reached out and grabbed the Bishop by his robe and said, "I like your dress, sweetie, but your purse in on fire."

One of the definitions of worship is "worthship", giving God his worth. I would like to give an additional definition of worship as it might apply to the Anglican Communion. "Worship is the attempt to create an atmosphere in which we can know God's love and make God's love known." In the Episcopal Church, "worship is the attempt to create an atmosphere in which we can know God's love and we can make God's love known."

In order to help you understand the definition I would like to offer the following illustration. A certain young man had been dating a special young woman for some time. He was in love with her. He decided it was time for him to propose to her. He wanted to pop the question. He invited her to his apartment so that he might propose to her, but before she arrived he wanted to set the atmosphere. So of course he thoroughly cleaned his apartment and dressed in his best suit for the occasion. He got out his finest dinnerware and prepared the finest meal he knew how to prepare. He chose an excellent wine. In order to prove to her that he was in fact a new male, a very sensitive sort of man, he put flowers on the table, lit candles, and went about his apartment spraying aromatic spray. He put some music on the stereo. When she arrived, they had some conversation. They talked about their life together, their journey together, if you will. Then at the appointed time he popped the question. He offered her a gold ring with a diamond in it. That ring was an outward and visible sign of his love for that girl.

**Anglican worship
creates an atmosphere
for the experience of God's love.**

Now if you can understand what goes into creating a romantic atmosphere for a man and woman then you can understand the role that ritual, symbolism and ceremony play in creating an atmosphere for the experience of God's love. Here these all work together in an effort to create an atmosphere which will appeal to all five senses – sight, sound, touch, taste, and smell.

I want to suggest three characteristics of worship that apply to worship in the Anglican Church. The first characteristic is that worship is a universal instinct. To worship is to be human and to be human is to worship. Worship is the consequence of not taking life and living for granted. When we begin to take life in God's wonderful universe for granted, we no longer need to worship. When we lose our sense of amazement, our sense of awe, our sense of thanksgiving for God and God's world then we have no need for worship. Worship is that wide-eyed approach to living that looks at life with amazement and awe. Worship is the ability to look at the things we see every day and often take for granted and respond, "This is the Lord's doing. It is marvelous to our eyes."

It has been suggested that when we ignore God all week or, in fact, for weeks on end, that we are going to have a very difficult time focusing on God on Sunday mornings. In fact, I've heard it illustrated that it would be easier for a person to go into Grand Central Station and try to find an old acquaintance he hasn't seen in years than it would be to try to go in a church and find God after ignoring God on a daily basis. To worship God with ease we have to practice loving God every day of our lives. To see God in worship we need to see God in the everyday, and if we see God in the everyday then we can see God better on Sunday.

The second thing that I'd like to suggest to you is that in the Episcopal Church worship is not a spectator sport. Worship is not for spectators. It is an aerobic activity. The liturgy is what we all do together. Priests are not entertainers. I don't play the piano and I don't sing very well, so I would make a rotten entertainer. The choir and the choirmaster are not here to entertain us. There is a critical distinction between worship in a liturgical church and worship in a nonliturgical church. The Episcopal worship service makes lousy television. You can't watch it. You have to participate in it and be a part of it. It's not just a matter of all of us coming together to sing a hymn or two and have the scripture reading, some prayers, a sermon and then tacking communion on the end. The Holy Eucharist, the Liturgy, is a great drama. It's a pageant. It's a play in which we are all participants. There's direction. There's movement. There's purpose. These all are designed to inspire and uplift us. But we are not the audience. God is the audience.

The Book of Common Prayer solidly ties us to the historic Catholic understanding of worship. The Book of Common Prayer is not an alternative service book. If you're going to be an Episcopalian you will use the Book of Common Prayer in the services of worship. The Book of Common Prayer, not doctrines and dogmas, symbolizes the unity of the Episcopal Church. The Eucharist itself is designed to require a response from us. You have to participate in the Eucharist. Your communion will not be brought to you. I've heard it said that there is no curb service in the Episcopal Church. I had to smile when an advertisement for a communion kit came across my desk. It was a disposable styrofoam tray containing little jelly cartons. The cartons are filled with grape juice. These would be hard to sell in the Episcopal Church. The Eucharist requires a response from us. We have to get up out of our pews and we have to go forward. We have to extend our hands. We have to reach for the body and blood of Christ. We have to take it. We have to want God's presence in our lives.

In the Eucharist we pray that Christ might be known to us in the breaking of the bread. In that sense the Lord's Supper is not a memorial meal. It is not a matter of getting together and remembering what a wonderful fellow Jesus was and thinking on all the fine things he did for us. The Holy Eucharist is the celebration of Christ's resurrected presence with us here and now. It is our Lord's own service. He becomes present to us in a special way, in a unique way. Here we ask Him to transform us, change us and make us new creations. Through the bread of heaven and the cup of salvation we ask that He might dwell in us and we in Him. Because the Holy Eucharist is a great mystery Episcopalians resist and even become hostile to any effort to introduce sentimentalism or anything that is faddish or cute to the service of communion. Our English heritage becomes very apparent when it comes to those things. The celebration of the Lord's supper shall be done with decency. And it shall be done with order.

The third and final characteristic I would like to suggest to you concerns the purpose of worship itself. Through worship we are to lose ourselves in adoration and praise of God. Occasionally someone will say to me, "You know, I came to church but I didn't get anything out of it." I understand what they are saying. I am even sympathetic on occasion. But let me suggest an alternative approach to worship. Let me suggest that we come to worship to lose ourselves. We come to empty ourselves so that God might make us full. If we find the various elements of worship distracting or ends in themselves, then we are going to be missing the mark. If we let something distract us, take our attention away from what we are doing, then we have missed the mark. I heard it described this way once. "If you have to count the steps, then you aren't dancing." That may be true of worship as well. If we have to concentrate on the very elements of worship, then we aren't worshiping. Worship is when we focus our attention on God. If that is to be our purpose then certain responsibilities are implied.

First, the priests, the choirs, the acolytes, the ushers all have a responsibility to the people. We have a responsibility to be well prepared. We have a responsibility to lead the congregation in worship and understand that our purpose is to point to God and not to be entertainers. We have a responsibility to call the people's attention to God and not call attention to ourselves. If we are to lead others in worship we must worship. We need to design a service through which God can uplift, inspire, which will make intimacy with God possible.

Second, the people have a responsibility to one another. Worshipers must be tolerant of one another's preferences. There is a tendency for all of us to value things according to our own subjective experience. If it was meaningful to me then it was a good thing. If it wasn't meaningful to me, then it's not a good thing. What is called for in worship is tolerance. What is meaningful to one may not be so to another. We have a responsibility to one another to participate in the worship. We come to do this together. We should respond to the liturgy with great openness. We will sing the hymns with much gusto. I heard someone say once, "I don't sing well. In fact, I don't sing at all." In those cases let's take some direction from the Bible. "Make a joyful noise." If we simply stand in a passive posture during the service of worship, we are first of all communicating that we are there to be entertained. Friends, if you come to church to be entertained you will be greatly disappointed. More important than that, we let our fellow worshipers down. Have you ever heard the old expression, "A chain is only as strong as its weakest link"? It applies to a congregation coming together for worship. Have you ever been a part of a task force or a production or a program or a committee in which members did not take their responsibility seriously? Have you ever had to carry it all alone because others didn't carry their share of the load? Remember what a draining experience that can be? We also know the incredible results that can be achieved when everybody is working together for one purpose. Consider the incredible results that could be achieved if every person gathered in a church building Sunday after Sunday did so with the singular purpose of worshiping God. Consider what can happen when we lose ourselves in the praise and adoration of God and everyone participates and everyone carries their part.

Finally, we have a responsibility to ourselves. We need to come to worship with a thirst for God. We need to come before God with a spirit of anticipation. Come with a sense of expectancy. Expect God to touch you in the service of worship, expect Jesus to make his presence known to you. Expect God to touch you through the service. At some instant, whether it's during a hymn or a prayer or the scriptures or the sermon or the communion itself, at some point expect God to touch you. Expect the Almighty to do so, and God will touch you.

When one of my sons was about three years old he was sitting in his highchair at the table. We were having hamburgers and potato chips. During the course of the dinner he took a potato chip off his tray. He lifted the potato chip up in front of his face and broke it into two pieces. He handed a piece to me and said, "the peace of God", and then he extended his arms to give me a hug and a kiss. Maybe that's a case of monkey see, monkey do. I choose to think it was the beginning of his understanding of the role of ritual, ceremony, and symbols in the expression of our love for one another and for our God.

I would never suggest to you that God needs our rituals, ceremonies, and symbols. That is readily apparent. What I will suggest to you is this. If we are to express to God and to one another our inner feelings, our inner thoughts, then we need ritual, ceremony, and symbol. God doesn't need them. But we do. I saw a bumper sticker that may best summarize all of this. "Join the Episcopal Church. Do random acts of kindness and senseless acts of beauty."

Do random acts of kindness

and

senseless acts of beauty

Chapter 7

ARE EPISCOPALIANS JUST A LOT OF DO-GOODERS?

The Bible teaches us that God created a garden. I think we miss that point sometimes. God created a garden for us to live in – a garden, a place of beauty, a garden, a place of peace and harmony, a place for us to play and to laugh and to love. In Eden God created a garden, a place of inspiration, a place for lovers, a place for children to discover. God created the garden of Eden so wonderful that it was called paradise and into our care the garden was entrusted. Now we live in a jungle! God gave us a garden. We live in a jungle! A jungle in which disease is rampant, a jungle in which little children go to bed at night with their bellies bloated from hunger, a jungle in which the various tribes hoard their wealth as though it were their own personal possession, a jungle in which the law is suspicion and hate,

**God gave us a garden.
We live in a jungle.**

where war is a constant threat, and the ultimate destruction of life as we know it is an everyday reality. We live in a jungle in which fear is our companion, tears our release, and defense the rallying cry. Think about that jungle. It was in that jungle that was once a garden that they crucified the saviour. His only crime was trying to point us back to the garden. He wanted to lead us back to the garden. There was a garden in that jungle in which there was an empty tomb. There they buried the body of Jesus. But early on that first Easter morning a woman was walking in that garden and she saw the risen Lord. He is alive! He lives to lead us back into the garden and out of the jungle. The Church is not the garden, but we exist to lead people out of the jungle and back to the garden. Let me propose some of the ways the Episcopal Church attempts to do this very thing.

Several years ago I was a member of an organization concerned about a piece of legislation being prepared for action by the Texas state legislature. The legislature invited the Executive Committee to appear before a select committee in Austin. Since I was a member of the Executive Committee, I got up early one Monday morning, caught a Southwest Airlines flight out of Dallas' Love Field for Austin. Since I was going directly from the airport to the state capitol, I wore my clerical collar. After the plane had taken off I began to thumb through the notes in my legal pad to organize my thoughts one more time before appearing before the committee. There was a gentleman sitting next to me. He asked, "Are you going to Austin to preach a sermon?" I told him, "No, I am going to Austin to appear before a committee of the state legislature." On hearing this he turned beet red. He exclaimed, "Why can't you preachers stick to soul saving? Why does the Church have to keep meddling in politics? Why don't you just stick to the spiritual things and leave the running of the country to the rest of us?"

**Our ministry is to point the way out of the jungle
and back to the garden.**

One of the recent rediscoveries of the Anglican Communion is that our Lord preached a very radical gospel. If we take a close look at Jesus' ministry and his teachings we will discover a gospel that is revolutionary, a radical gospel, a gospel that demands a response from us. One of the first things that we can learn about God's view of the world from Jesus' teaching and his ministry is that God is not just interested in religion. God is interested in the entire universe. God is interested in those things that we would deem spiritual and those things that we would deem secular.

Jesus did not limit himself to soul saving. Jesus ministered to the total person. The healing miracles of Jesus are not proofs of his divinity. They are manifestations of his humanity, a humanity at harmony with God. Let us not forget that Jesus fed the multitudes not to prove that he was divine, but he fed the multitudes because in his humanity he had compassion on them. They were hungry. Jesus healed the sick not to prove anything to anyone but because he had compassion on them in their illness. Jesus became a companion to the outcast because they were lonely and for no other reason. Jesus taught us to pray, "Our Father". Our Father, not My Father, not My personal Father, but Our Father so that we all would understand that we are brothers and sisters under one God. In the garden, in God's family "there is neither Jew nor Greek, neither male nor female, neither slave nor free," but all of us are his beloved children. In the jungle hatred, revenge, prejudice are the law. The pathway back to the garden is marked forgiveness, compassion, understanding.

John the Baptist was in prison. He sent his disciples to ask Jesus, "Are you the one or are we to expect another?" Jesus said, "Go back to John and tell him what you yourselves see and hear. Tell him that the blind receive sight, the lame walk, the lepers are cleansed, the deaf hear, the dead are raised up, and the poor have the gospel preached to them."

On another occasion Jesus spoke to them in parables. He said to them, "Come, blessed of my Father, inherit the kingdom which has been prepared for you since the beginning of the ages. For I was hungry and you gave me food. I was thirsty and you gave me drink. I was a stranger and you welcomed me. I was naked and you clothed me. I was sick and you visited me. I was in prison and you came to me." And the people all asked, "Lord, when did we see you hungry and feed you? Lord, when did we see you naked and clothed you?" Jesus responded, "For as much as you have done it unto one of the least of these my brethren, you have done it unto me."

We learn from Jesus that the work of the church is the work of Jesus. If we limit ourselves only to soul saving then we have but half the gospel. If we limit ourselves to just the doing of good works, then we misunderstand our mission. For our ministry is to point the way out of the jungle and back to the garden.

A little over thirty years ago the Episcopal Church was being led by a Presiding Bishop I consider one of the greatest prophets of our day. That Presiding Bishop moved the Episcopal Church to respond to the radical gospel of Jesus with new vigor and new vitality. Our Church began to speak prophetically in the jungle, which was filled with human anguish. Our Church spoke, "Thus saith the Lord: A person's value, worth, and character in life shall not be determined by the color of their skin." And to a war which our country had not declared nor to which it was committed to win, our Church spoke prophetically. "Thus saith the Lord, The daily slaughter of our young men must cease." Our Church began to organize ministries to respond to the radical demands of the gospel. Our Church moved that never again would half of the membership of the Episcopal Church be considered second-class citizens. We opened our ordained ministries to include women. And to those who had suffered the trauma of divorce our Church reconsidered its ministry to the divorced person. For the hungry we began to organize soup kitchens, for those who sleep under bridges and in cardboard boxes at night we began to organize street ministries, and for the poor and the elderly we began to provide housing. Our Church continues to speak prophetically in an effort to control nuclear madness. The Episcopal Church has led the way in speaking prophetically on behalf of all persons considered to be modern day outcasts.

Responding to the radical demands of the gospel costs us. I believe that some of the one million members we lost in a single decade can be traced to our prophetic ministries. But the Lord has blessed the Episcopal Church in other ways. Giving to the Episcopal Church tripled in that same period. In other words, those who stayed were giving three times as much. Today the Anglican Communion is one of the fastest growing branches of Christ's Church in the world. What we Anglicans have come to understand is this. We can't, Sunday after Sunday, pray for the hungry, the poor, the sick, the elderly, and peace of the world without doing something to address those needs.

The Episcopal Church is organized into dioceses. Ideally that keeps us from turning in on ourselves. It helps us understand that we are a part of a church that is much larger than any single congregation. We are a part of a worldwide fellowship. A substantial part of every dollar placed in an Episcopal offering plate will go to work outside the congregation. It will go to the work of the diocese and the national church. From the Navajo reservations to the inner city. It will support the mission congregations in our own diocese. Monies will go to support ministries from China to the Caribbean. If you go around this nation you will find Episcopal congregations large and small involved in day care centers, opening their facilities for Alcoholics Anonymous, literacy programs and day shelters for the homeless. Episcopalians are not just a bunch of do-gooders. They're just simply attempting to respond to the radical demands of the gospel.

The Anglican Communion is composed of a people concerned about the well-being of all of our society. While heaven is our destination, we strive not to be so heavenly-minded that we are of no earthly good. Not only must we respond to the real needs of those God presents to us, but we are committed to the transformation of society. The Episcopal Church believes society can be transformed. We do not have to be content to live in the jungle with its violence, fear, disease, and warfare. We strive to transform individuals. Transformed individuals will transform society. One cannot become a new person in our understanding and be content to reside in the jungle. A transformed person longs to return to the garden and to bring all people with them.

Why don't we just stick to soul saving? We can't. The Church can't. God created a garden. We live in a jungle. We exist to point the way back to the garden. The gospel of Jesus cannot be limited to soul saving. It cannot be limited to "spiritual things". In fact, the gospel of Jesus cannot be limited at all.

The Episcopal Church is a Bible Church.

Chapter 8

WHY DO EPISCOPALIANS REJECT BIBLICAL FUNDAMENTALISM?

Episcopalians are often put on the defensive when it comes to our approach to the Scriptures. What often is implied is that we Episcopalians don't teach the Bible. Since we don't teach the Bible, we don't understand the Bible. The judgment is that if we did understand the Bible we would change some of our ways. From time to time I'll see a church advertise itself as a Bible church. The implication is that there are some non-Bible churches. Not too long ago, I saw a church advertise itself as the "Open Bible Church". Again, the antithesis of an open Bible church is a closed Bible church.

I want to remind you of some of the things you need to remember about the Anglican Communion and our use of the scriptures.

First, I want to remind you that it was the Anglican Communion, the Church of England, that gave the Bible to the English speaking world. It was the Church of England that translated the Scriptures into the vernacular. The English speaking world received the scriptures from us.

The second thing I would remind you is that in the Episcopal Church, in the Anglican Communion, absolutely nothing can be taught as being necessary to one's salvation that cannot be found in the scriptures.

Third, I would remind you that every deacon, priest, and bishop who wants to be ordained in the Episcopal Church must take an oath of conformity. This is the Oath of Conformity: "I do believe that the Old and New Testaments are the word of God and contain all things necessary for one's salvation."

Fourth, the normal Sunday in the Episcopal Church, when we celebrate a full service of Holy Communion, one hears read three lessons from scripture, and a Psalm. There normally is a lesson from the Old Testament, an Epistle, a Gospel reading, and a selection from the Psalter.

The last thing that I would remind you is that clergy and laity who are faithful to the lectionary of morning and evening prayer, over the course of two years would read the major portions of the Bible, including the Apocrypha.

The point is this. The Episcopal Church is very much a Bible church. The reason Holy Communion is our primary act of worship is that we are a Bible church. We recognize the prominence of the Lord's own service in the lives of those New Testament Christians. The Holy Eucharist was celebrated on the first day of every week. Our bishops are an apostolic order because we are a Bible church. We anoint the sick, practice the laying on of hands, and maintain the sacraments of confession because we are a Bible church. We are a Bible church, but we are not the type of Bible church that phrase usually conjures up.

We're not Biblical literalists. We do not practice proof texting. We do not take every word of the Bible literally. For example, should we take literally the Book of Exodus, "If you lend money to any of my people with you who is poor, you shall not be to him as a creditor and you shall not exact interest from him." Personally, I hope to find a literalistic banker somewhere. I might get a nice loan at no interest because the Bible says so.

Episcopalians don't surface-read the scriptures. We don't begin with an opinion or with a particular point of view and then try to find a scripture text to substantiate it. There is a true story about a congregation that was building a new Christian Education building. They wanted to put a scripture passage appropriate to each Sunday School classroom above the door. So above the youth room they wrote these words from Psalm 71: "O God, from my youth thou has taught me." Above the senior citizens' classroom door, they copied from Job 32, "Let the days speak and many years teach wisdom." When it came to the baby nursery they had a great deal of difficulty finding a passage of scripture to put above the nursery door. They found one in the fifteenth chapter of 1st Corinthians. They wrote this above the baby nursery door: "We shall not all sleep, but we shall all be changed"!

The fact of the matter is that we <u>can</u> find a verse of scripture to substantiate just about any point of view or any opinion. I think we're too quickly impressed by people who can quote scripture. I want to remind you of something, and I hope that you'll never forget it. Satan, the Devil, can quote scripture! In the temptations of Jesus in the wilderness the gospel writers report that the Devil himself quoted scripture in order to tempt our Lord. The Devil himself quoted scripture! We are too quickly impressed by those who can quote the Bible. Throughout history the scriptures have been quoted to justify harsh attitudes toward the poor and the unemployed. The scriptures have been quoted to keep women in subservient roles in the church and in society. Do you remember the scriptures that were quoted in an effort to defeat John Kennedy when he was running for President of the United States? Or do you remember Pope John the Twenty-Third and the scriptures that were quoted to label him as the anti-Christ? Episcopalians don't begin with a preconceived idea and try to find a scripture to support it. Episcopalians don't begin with an opinion and then look in the Bible to find something to substantiate it.

Proof texting and Biblical literalism are the cornerstones of the fundamentalistic movement. It is a movement that is relatively new in the history of Christianity. In fact, it started in 1910 with the publication of a series of books, twelve books to be exact, entitled "The Fundamentals – A Testimony of the Truth". Since 1910, fundamentalism has primarily swept through the Baptist and the Presbyterian Churches bringing painful divisions to those two great

Christian groups. Fundamentalism has never been a success in the Episcopal Church, nor is it likely to be. We have a hierarchical system of authority. In order for fundamentalism to succeed, it appears that congregationalism has to be the form of government, and, individual beliefs must be given greater merit than historical Christianity.

We believe in divine inspiration.
We do not believe in divine dictation.

We Episcopalians reject fundamentalism for several reasons.

First, we believe in divine inspiration. We do not believe in divine dictation. Episcopalians believe that the Bible was written by men who were divinely inspired, but they were not stenographers in a trance. Before we can understand what the Bible means we have to first understand who wrote it, to whom it was written, the culture of the people, and the situation to which the writer was addressing himself. We recognize that the Bible was an evolutionary product. It evolved! As the gospels and letters were circulated, other writers would edit or make additions in order to serve their own purposes. Hence, Episcopalians hold that the Bible is divinely inspired, but not divinely dictated.

Second, Anglicans do not believe that the Bible is a single book. The Bible is a library and each book has to be approached individually. One does not read poetry with the same eyes that one would use to read a biography. Nor does one read literature with the same eyes used to read an epistle. Do you realize that not even the followers of Judaism put equal weight on all of the books of the Old Testament? They consider certain portions of the Old Testament more holy than others. Remember it was their book first. Or did you know that Christians through the centuries have actually disputed which books ought to be included in the Bible? For example, did you know that Esther does not even mention God? Did you know that many of the Protestant reformers wanted the Book of James removed from the Bible? Did you know that the Book of Revelation is the last book in the new Testament because the Bishops in council had a tough time deciding whether or not even to include it? Don't you think that John is superior to Judges, or Corinthians is superior to Chronicles? If you still think all the books of the Bible have equal merit, when is the last time you tried to wade through the Book of Leviticus? The canon of scripture was closed four hundred years after the birth of Christ. The Bible is the Bible because the Church says it is the Bible.

The third reason that we Anglicans reject Biblical fundamentalism is that we insist that the Bible be treated with the same quality of scholarship and respect that we would treat any other book. We believe that reading the scriptures apart from reason is incredibly dangerous. When we cease to use our minds in Bible study, individual opinions and individual interpretations are given the authority of God. The question that we must bring to the scriptures is not what this particular passage of scripture means to me, but what did it mean to the history and mission of God's people? It's critical that we not ask of the Bible questions it was never designed to answer. The Bible is a book of faith. It is not a book of science. When we bring biblical scholarship and critical analysis to scriptural studies, truth is not threatened nor is truth compromised, but we can discover truth in even greater depth.

When we bring critical study and scholarship to the scriptures we begin to learn that Samson is not the story of a man with muscles, but it's a story of a Nazarite priest and his role and his function in the community. When we bring Biblical scholarship and critical analysis to the scriptures, we find that the challenge is not to discern whether Jonah swallowed the whale or the whale swallowed Jonah, but that the book of Jonah was written to remind the people of Israel that they were to preach Yahweh in all parts of the world, even to a sin city like Ninevah. When we bring Biblical scholarship to the scriptures, we learn that the story of the wise men is not the story of gifts of gold, frankincense, and myrrh, but the story of all races of mankind kneeling in worship before the one true God. We learn that if we are to understand Pentecost we have to contrast it with the Tower of Babel. If we want to understand Golgotha, we have to contrast it to Passover. If we want to understand the feeding of the multitudes, we have to contrast it to the institution of the Holy Eucharist. If we want to understand the mission of the new Israel, we contrast it with the mission of the Old Israel. And if we want to understand heaven and hell, we've got to understand Eden.

The fourth reason that we Anglicans reject Biblical fundamentalism is that we understand that Christianity is not faith in a book, but in a person. The purpose of the Bible is to point to Jesus. Too often the Bible is used as a stumbling block, a club, or a shield to drive away from Christ the very people we're trying to bring near to him. When the Bible becomes the primary object of one's faith, it becomes idolatrous. In fact, we call it Bibliolatry. The risen Christ is the source and object of our faith, not the Bible. It is Jesus who saves, not scripture verses. Martin Luther said, "The Bible is like the manger. It is not Jesus Christ, but it contains Christ."

It has been said that the average adult has a twelve year old's understanding of the scriptures. I'd really like to think that's not true, but just in case it is, I want to suggest a method of Bible study. First, begin with the Bible. Don't begin with an opinion, a preconceived idea, and then look in the Bible. Begin with the Bible and find out what the Bible has to say. Begin with a good translation of the Bible. Now this is a pastoral opinion. You can take it for that. No Living Bibles or other paraphrases! The Living Bible, in my opinion, is not at all helpful in our efforts to understand the scripture. The Living Bible is not a Bible at all. It is, in fact, a paraphrase. It is one man's opinion of what the Bible ought to say. So if you're going to study the Bible, begin with the Bible. Get a good translation. Second, seek to understand the Bible in light of tradition and history. Utilize the very best academic tools that you have at your disposal. Use good scholarship in your study of the Bible. Try to understand the words, if you can, in the languages in which they were written. Try to find out who wrote the particular passage you are studying. Learn about the culture to which he wrote and try to find out the reason that he was writing. A good Bible commentary is absolutely essential. And last, seek to understand the Bible in the light of reason.

Beware of those who would equate faith with blindness and superstition. Faith is a relationship. It is not a series of dogmas. In good Biblical study questions are encouraged.

Beware of those who would treat the Bible as though it were a single book in which you have to believe all of it or you can't believe any of it. The Bible is a library and it needs to be approached as a library.

Beware of those who would teach that which intuitively and historically you know to be incorrect. God gave us brains to think and hearts with which to listen, and we need to use them when it comes to Biblical study. Again, the third person of the Holy Trinity is the Holy Spirit, not the Holy Scriptures.

Beware of those who would use the Bible as a club in order to beat down all other forms of knowledge. We Anglicans certainly believe the Bible should be taught, but it's not the only thing that should be taught. God speaks to us through other things.

Beware of those who would use the Bible to bring division to the body of Christ, those who would use the Bible to pit Christian against Christian or to suggest in any way that they have cornered the God market. Jesus prayed that all His Church might be one.

And beware of those who use the Bible to justify hatred or prejudice in any form. The Bible is a love story, a love story between God and man. God has given us the scriptures. God continues to speak to us through them. At its very best, the Bible reminds us where we have been, who we are, and where we are going.

ARE THERE ANY EPISCOPALIANS IN HEAVEN?

Someone once asked the Reverend John Jenkins when he was rector of Trinity Church in New Orleans, Louisiana, "Do Episcopalians believe in the second coming of Jesus Christ?" Father Jenkins thought for just a moment before answering. "Yes, they do. They just don't want him to come this weekend because they have a great party planned and it would be a shame to have to cancel it." You know, we Episcopalians have been the target of a lot of ridicule regarding our rather cavalier attitude towards life and the judgment of God.

John Shelby (This Hebrew lad Mary, the Guelwets always die)

Bishop Jack Spong in his book *The Easter Moment* records the time that he was debating with one of his Protestant friends over the five commandments of Puritanism. The five commandments of Puritanism are: "Thou shalt not smoke. Though shalt not drink. Thou shalt not dance. Thou shalt not play cards. Thou shalt not go to the movies." They were debating whether or not God would hold all those things against Episcopalians since we seem to take them rather lightly. It appeared that they were not going to be able to come to any kind of conclusion, so the Protestant minister offered a compromise. He said, "Well, let's just agree that we're all trying to get to the same place." Bishop Spong said he could agree to that but he thought that we Episcopalians were having a little more fun getting there.

Episcopalians hold that heaven is a promise. Heaven is one of the promises of God. It is much more than just a pipe dream. It is a promise. Are there any words more comforting in all of scripture at the time of death than these words of Jesus? "Let not your hearts be troubled. Neither let them be afraid. Ye believe in God. Believe also in me. For in my Father's house are many mansions. If it were not so I would have told you. And I go to prepare a place for you and if I go to prepare a place for you, I will come again and receive you unto myself so that where I am there you might be also."

For the Episcopalian, the service of Holy Communion is a service of meeting. It is a place where we gather with all of the communion of saints, those who are known to us and those who are unknown to us. With them we can lift our voices in prayer and praise to God in the great fellowship of the saints. The scriptures describe the fellowship and the communion of saints as a great cloud of witnesses – a cloud of witnesses that surrounds us. When we pray and praise God, when we make Eucharist, we do it in communion with them. We do it in fellowship with them. In the Episcopal Church every Sunday is Easter. Every Sunday we celebrate the resurrection of Jesus Christ and we celebrate the fact that because He lives, we shall live as well. The resurrection of Jesus is a constant reminder to us that heaven is our destiny. Heaven is our ultimate home.

One of the great sadnesses of Christianity is that the promise of heaven has become a source of division and debate within the Church. The debate has raged for centuries as to who is going to get to go to heaven and who isn't going to get to go to heaven. It's ironic. It's as though we're the ones who are going to decide who gets to go to heaven and who doesn't, and not the Lord. There are those who would tell us that unless we subscribe to their particular denominational prescription for salvation, then we are doomed.

We can get so heavenly-minded
that we neglect making this world a better place

There's the very familiar story of St. Peter taking some new arrivals around heaven. He was showing them about the place when they came upon a group of people who were involved in a great prayer meeting. The guests asked, "St. Peter, who are these people?" He said, "Oh, these are the Baptists. They're having a prayer meeting here in heaven." They went a bit further and discovered those having a great preaching service and again asked, "Who are these?" And St. Peter responded, "These are the Methodists. They're having a preaching service." They walked along just a little bit further when they came to a great room, but the doors were all shut and sealed tight and there was a "Do Not Disturb" sign hanging on the doors. St. Peter put his finger over his lip and whispered, "Be quiet. In here are those of the denominations that think they are the only ones up here."

Episcopalians believe that the promise of heaven was given to us not to make us feel good about ourselves. Nor is it our task to pass judgment on those who are going to make it or those won't. But heaven is God's promise and it's something for us to celebrate. In the Prayer Book we remember all who have died in the communion of the church and those whose faith is known to God alone.

Karl Marx said that religion could become the opiate of the people. There's a sense in which that is entirely true. On the old television series M*A*S*H, there is a priest portrayed by the name of Father Mulcahy. What I'm going to describe to you is the Father Mulcahy syndrome. Father Mulcahy is very heavenly-minded, but in the M*A*S*H situation he is of absolutely no earthly good. He is a nice guy, but his ministry is somewhat like pablum and his counsel somewhat like sugar pills. There's a danger. The danger is that we can put so much emphasis on the heavenly that we take a passive attitude towards the earthly. We can become so consumed with saving people's souls so that they can go to heaven that we forget about saving their lives here on earth. We can get so heavenly-minded that we neglect making this world a better place to live. I find most frightening those extremists who would use the promise of heaven to negate the value of life on earth. There are those who take a rather fatalistic approach towards death and war. There are those who would even tell us that nuclear destruction is a part of God's plan to herald in the apocalyptic age.

We Anglicans believe that our resurrected life begins here on earth. It begins with our baptism. It is something that we can celebrate here and in the hereafter. Here on earth we can have friendship with God. Here on earth we can enjoy the abundant life. Here and now we can know the peace which passes all understanding.

Matthew 5:1-11 contains some of the most familiar teachings of Jesus. We call them the beatitudes. The word "blessed" is a very difficult word to translate. In fact, the contemporary word for "blessed" is "happy". "Happy are those" or even better, "Congratulations". Congratulations to the poor in spirit. Congratulations to those who are weak and vulnerable in the eyes of the world for they know their need of God. Congratulations to those of you who mourn. Congratulations to those of you who have lost a loved one in death. You are in a better position to open your hearts and your minds to God's word and be touched by his spirit than those who are unfamiliar with grief. Congratulations to those of you who are merciful, for your hearts have been cleansed of hatred and revenge and judgmentalism and you have been set free. Congratulations to those of you who have been persecuted for Jesus' sake, for your sense of right and wrong is not dependent upon your popularity or on the public opinion polls. Your sense of right and wrong is dependent upon your devotion to God.

The promise of heaven reminds us that we are a people on a journey and as such we are called to grow, to change, and to mature. The secret bliss of heaven will be found in a perfect relationship with God. Heaven, then, is not a reward, but a result! An unholy person would find heaven intolerable. An unholy person would really not want to be there. So hell is more a sense of eternal loss than eternal punishment. The fires of hell are fueled both here and in the hereafter by the human heart that is consumed with anger, bitterness, stubbornness, greed, and all of the other manifestations of a self-centered life. The gospel of Jesus Christ was given to transform us, to change us from glory into glory. In Christ we are to become new creatures. In Christ we are to become a new creation. It is through the power of the resurrected Christ that Simon, the coward, became Peter, the rock. It is through the power of the resurrected Christ that Saul, the persecutor, became Paul, the apostle. It is through the power of the resurrected Christ that Augustine, the lust-filled, became St. Augustine. Heaven is the destiny of saints, and Jesus Christ is in the business of transforming men and women into the saints of God. Perhaps the most familiar saint of all expressed this best in the prayer that is attributed to him. I speak of the Prayer of St. Francis. God grant us the grace to offer this prayer with our hearts and to respond to it with our lives.

Lord, make us instruments of your peace.
Where there is hatred, let us sow love.
Where there is injury, pardon;
Where there is discord, union;

Where there is doubt, faith;
Where there is despair, hope;
Where there is darkness, light;
Where there is sadness, joy.

Grant that we might not seek so much
to be consoled as to console;
to be understood as to understand;
to be loved as to love.

For it is in giving that we receive;
It is in pardoning that we are pardoned;
And it is in dying that we are born
to eternal life.

Chapter 10

THE EPISCOPAL CHURCH WELCOMES YOU

As we entered Trinity Cathedral in Columbia, South Carolina for the opening service of the Diocesan Convention, I noticed a couple of people standing outside the Cathedral gates with signs. "Repent," proclaimed one. Another quoted the Bible condemning adultery, divorce, homosexuals, and others "beyond the pale". My eyes shot from those signs to the one permanently positioned on the Cathedral grounds. That sign was the familiar red, white, and blue one that reads simply, "The Episcopal Church Welcomes You."

My thoughts went back to those signs: the two signs filled with judgment and condemnation and the third which simply proclaimed "Welcome". Welcome, all of you! Welcome, those of you who carry sins so secret and so devastating that you fear ever being completely forgiven. Welcome, those of you who are prisoners of your own secrets. Welcome, those of you who carry hate in your hearts for your brother, sister, mother, father. Welcome, those of you who are confused in any way and beaten down with guilt. Welcome, those of you who have gone to this House of Worship or another and received not mercy, but condemnation. Welcome, those of you who have been so wounded by your own sins or the sins of others that you need to feel the solace of the Heavenly Father. Welcome, those of you who are so wearied by the changes and chances of this transitory life that you need to rest in the presence of the Eternal.

I fully realize that there is a need in the world for the Church to hold up the plumb line of God. There are standards against which we must measure our behavior. However, this prophetic role need not be fulfilled with such delight. It cannot be said too often or too forcefully: sin is a disease to be healed, not a crime to be punished. If anything stands out in the Gospels it is the compassion and love that Our Lord showed the repentant. If God is calling the Episcopal

Church to be that branch of His Body that places love above judgment and proclamation over prophecy, then it may well be the role that we need to embrace with enthusiasm. The voices reminding us of our sinfulness and need to condemn are indeed plentiful. They lift their signs high and with great delight. The voice that those broken by their own sinfulness and the sins of others need to hear is not filled with pietistic judgmentalism, but with compassion, mercy, and love. Perhaps God is calling us to bid His welcome to those who would not feel welcomed any place else. After all, who was it who said, "Come unto me, all ye that are weary and heavy-laden, and I will give you rest?" *The Episcopal Church Welcomes You.* All of you.

Chapter 11

I AM IN LOVE

From time to time I read of those who have given up on the Episcopal Church. I hear of those who can take no more. There is a part of me that understands what they are saying and on occasion empathizes with them, but I have a problem. I am in love! I am in love with the Episcopal Church.

I love this Church's determination to balance scripture, tradition, and reason. I love her majestic worship, the mystery of her sacraments, and the emphasis on God's love and forgiveness. I love her courage to stand up to the forces of bigotry and to fight for the equality of all people. I love her sensitivity to the poor, the sick, and the needy. I love her great hymns that have outlived the catchy jingles and campfire songs of every generation. I love to see the clergy all dressed in their finery.

I am still moved by the singing of the Venite, the Benedicite, and the Magnificat. Morning Prayer, the Great Litany, and Evensong are pressed into my soul. I like seeing the altar prepared for communion, the brass polished, the flowers lovingly arranged, and the smell of incense on occasion. The familiar prayers of the Prayer Book bring me comfort and are a welcome part of my life. Each Christmas Eve I pray that it will not be the last time I light a candle, kneel in the darkness, and sing *Silent Night*.

Oh, I do get angry with this Church of ours. I often wonder if those in authority have lost touch with reality. I have come to fear the religion section of the newspaper lest there be another article on my beloved Church that puts us in the most unfavorable light. I pray hardest when the Bishops gather, and pray harder still when the General Convention meets. I fear which special interest group shall prevail, and I wonder just how many more storms this old ship can endure before she does, in fact, fragment.

I do not like all that she does. I do not agree with all who attempt to speak for her. There are many times I feel very much out of step with the rest of the band, and on occasion I resist the newest set of marching orders. But leave her? Leave the Episcopal Church? Leave the Church of my conversion, confirmation, ordination? No, as far afield as she may go on occasion, I could not leave her. I love this wonderful Church. I want to spend the rest of my life in her bosom, die in her arms, and have the faithful remember me in their prayers. No, I shall never leave her. It's love, honest to God love, and I can't walk away from that.

POSTLOGUE

It is really quite presumptuous for any one member of the Episcopal Church to try to speak for the Church as a whole. The Anglican Communion is a large and diverse community. Still, each time we preach a sermon or teach an inquirers class, we do that very thing. Obviously, we always teach from our perspective and within our experience of a particular portion of this Church.

Since the Anglican Communion is not a confessional church, we are left to the lex orandi – lex credendi in our efforts to define ourselves to others. From the time of the formal separation from Rome in the sixteenth century we have been left to the task of balancing our identity between historic catholic Christianity and the various movements of the reformation and post-reformation period. The various revisions of the English Prayer Book and our own American Prayer Book reflect this effort. Some members of our communion have been more comfortable attempting to maintain the elements of the historic catholic faith while others have found greater expression by integrating the various aspects of post-reformation and contemporary Christian movements.

To say that we are a Church in process in easily documented. Perhaps it is the reality of the process itself that is the most distinguishing mark of Anglicanism. The evidence of this process is readily apparent in the actions of Lambeth Conferences, General Conventions, Pastoral Letters, and the revisions of our Prayer Book and Hymnal.

These chapters have been this priest's effort to interpret those various actions. The overall objective is not the defense of Anglicanism, nor is it my intention to compare Anglicanism to other branches of Christ's Church. Hopefully, these chapters will enable both members and inquirers to better comprehend the Anglican process.

My greatest learning in writing these chapters is that as a priest I have often been guilty of answering questions that people are not even asking. I commend the many excellent resources to the inquirer who wants to know more about Anglican Church history, theology, and liturgy. The preceding chapters are dedicated to answering some of the most frequently asked questions this priest has received from inquirers. This is not intended to be a comprehensive study of Anglicanism.

Faithfully,
Dennis Maynard